Body Dysmorphia

*An Essential Guide
to Understanding
and Overcoming Body
Dysmorphic Disorder*

by Judy Stromberg

Table of Contents

Introduction 1

Chapter 1: Causes and Symptoms of Body Dysmorphic Disorder 7

Chapter 2: How BDD Is Diagnosed 17

Chapter 3: Behavioral Treatment Techniques and Medications 21

Chapter 4: Home Therapies and Interventions 27

Chapter 5: Self-Assessment of BDD 39

Chapter 6: Choosing an Appropriate Therapist 45

Chapter 7: Additional Tips for Coping with the Disorder 51

Conclusion 59

Introduction

Body Dysmorphic Disorder (BDD) or dysmorphophobia is categorized as a chronic mental illness or anxiety disorder characterized by extreme concern about one's own physical appearance. The person is so conscious of her physical flaws that it will impact all aspects of her. She fears going out and interacting with other people because she irrationally worries they might notice her minor flaws, which she believes are enormous ones.

If you have BDD, your social life, career, family and interpersonal relationships will suffer. You even tend to neglect your responsibilities because you have a different priority in terms of worrying about your appearance. Even that you know nobody is perfect, you simply cannot disregard the minor imperfections that you have. You stare at the mirror for hours, trying to figure out what you can do to hide, minimize, or modify that perceived imperfection.

Well I'm here to give you some good news: There are specific techniques you can implement that will gradually get rid of your dysmorphophobia. Since it's considered a mental and anxiety disorder, the treatment spans along the lines of Cognitive Behavior

Therapy and other similar behavioral adjustment methods.

This book is designed to provide you with important information that will help you overcome Body Dysmorphic Disorder. It is also an essential guide to understanding your disorder better so that you are better equipped to deal with it properly and effectively. What are you waiting for? Let's get started.

© Copyright 2015 by Miafn LLC—All rights reserved.

This document is geared towards providing reliable information in regards to the topic and issue covered. The publication is sold with the idea that the publisher is not required to render accounting, officially permitted, or otherwise, qualified services. If advice is necessary, legal or professional, a practiced individual in the profession should be ordered.

From a Declaration of Principles which was accepted and approved equally by a Committee of the American Bar Association and a Committee of Publishers and Associations.

In no way is it legal to reproduce, duplicate, or transmit any part of this document in either electronic means or in printed format. Recording of this publication is strictly prohibited and any storage of this document is not allowed unless with written permission from the publisher. All rights reserved.

The information provided herein is stated to be truthful and consistent, in that any liability, in terms of inattention or otherwise, by any usage or abuse of any policies, processes, or directions contained within is solely and completely the responsibility of the recipient reader. Under no circumstances will any legal responsibility or blame be held against the publisher for any reparation, damages, or monetary loss due to the information herein, either directly or indirectly.

Respective authors own all copyrights not held by the publisher.

The information herein is offered for informational purposes solely, and is universal as so. The presentation of the information is without contract or any type of guarantee assurance.

The trademarks that are used are without any consent, and the publication of the trademark is without permission or backing by the trademark owner. All trademarks and brands within this book are for clarifying purposes only and are the owned by the owners themselves, not affiliated with this document.

Chapter 1: Causes and Symptoms of Body Dysmorphic Disorder

The cause of Body Dysmorphic Disorder (BDD) has not yet been established specifically, however, clinicians have observed that the disorder appears commonly in persons who are in early adolescence. In relation to this, the early diagnosis of BDD can save lives and allow people with the disorder to cope with it more effectively. Individuals with BDD have been reported to have the following risk factors:

1. **Genes**

    It has been observed that people with BDD usually come from a family who has a history of the condition. Hence, experts concluded that genes inherited from parents can be a potential cause of the disorder.

2. **Brain abnormality**

    It was reported that persons with BDD have a brain structure that was different from that of a normal person. There is abnormal production or secretion of serotonin, the hormone responsible in nerve transmission to the brain. This is discussed more in Chapter 2.

3. **Environment**

   The culture and practices of the environment in which the person lived in can also be a root cause of the mental disorder. If the culture that the person grew in focuses on physical appearance as the most important aspect of an individual's personality, then the desire to appear perfect will dominate the person's mentality.

4. **Age**

   Young people in their early adolescence are more prone to BDD. This is because at this stage, they are in the process of seeking acceptance and belongingness. Also, this is the age when they try to gain self-confidence and establish their own identities.

5. **Abuse during childhood**

   Studies have revealed that some individuals who acquired BDD have been physically, verbally or sexually abused or bullied during their childhood. This aspect must be considered when finding the root cause of the BDD, so that appropriate measures or therapy strategies can be adopted.

6. **Lack of self-worth or self-confidence**

   One documented cause of BDD is lack of self-worth. The person feels that she is worthless because of her perceived flaws. This will turn her into an insecure person with no self-confidence. But if you observe the defects she is so concerned about, you'll notice that they are trivial (bushy eyebrows, grizzly hair or a pimple head). But the person with the disorder believes that these are immense flaws that turn her into a "monster".

The combination of these causative factors contributes to a person acquiring BDD.

Based on the Diagnostic and Statistical Manual of Mental Disorders and other scientific criteria given by other experts, the symptoms of BDD are the following:

Symptoms of BDD

1. **Extreme consciousness of one's physical appearance**

   The person is extremely conscious of small flaws in her physical appearance, and focuses on them. She takes long hours trying to "fix" those perceived flaws. Though nobody notices them, she's extremely uncomfortable with these minor defects.

2. **Significant impairment in psychosocial functioning**

   Because of this extreme consciousness of how she looks, she isolates herself from everyone and avoids socializing. She stays home to hide her imagined imperfection. This affects her psychosocial functions with regard to her family, friends and colleagues.

3. **Depression**

   Depression eventually sets in when the person cannot overcome their feelings of inadequacy and inferiority. This is a red alert stage because this depression can lead to more serious symptoms, such as aggression and suicide.

4. **Compulsive skin picking**

    This is usually done to remove or improve whatever the person believes as her skin imperfection. Apparently, she believes that picking her skin will make it smoother.

5. **Suicidal tendencies**

    The depression can escalate to suicidal tendencies that can endanger the life of the person. This is most applicable to adolescents who are struggling in establishing their identities.

6. **Aggression and violent behavior**

    The aggressive and violent behavior is caused by several factors, such as persistent dissatisfaction of surgical results, frustration about their perceived "deformity", anger at being a monster, and anger at being rejected (in their minds) by people around them. Even when they are accepted, they still think that people are not sincere in accepting them.

7. **Mirror conscious**

   The person looks at the mirror several times a day, more than necessary. On the other hand, she may also have utter dislike of looking at herself in the mirror. She is so preoccupied with her appearance that she becomes anxious and distressed.

8. **Undergoing aesthetic surgery various times**

   Since she believes that there's always something wrong with her looks, she tends to undergo aesthetic surgery various times to "correct' her imagined physical defects.

9. **Excessive vanity/grooming**

   She grooms herself excessively; applying her make-up several times; changing her hairstyle for no apparent reason, and "correcting" all unnecessary things that most people normally ignore. She is so vain that people are no longer pleased with her behavior. Her vanity is no longer normal.

10. Excessive diet and exercise

She goes on excessive fasting spells and rigorous exercises that can be life-threatening.

11. Focuses on minor flaws of her body and her appearance

When she finds a pimple, she picks at it and doesn't stop until she "eliminates" it. An out of place strand of hair will bother her until it has been tucked carefully; and even then, she will still "fix" her hair continuously.

12. Continuously compares herself with others

She has the habit of continuously comparing herself with others, and always noticing her imperfections, no matter how small they may be.

13. Constant thoughts of ugliness or deformity

The person constantly thinks that she is ugly or deformed, and that she looks like a monster.

14. Unwarranted changing of clothes

As part of her compulsive excessive grooming mentioned earlier, she's also so overly conscious of the clothes she wears that she irrationally keeps changing them, no matter how good they look on her.

These are the symptoms of BDD. If you notice, the actions are usually repetitive and can lead to inflicting injury on the body. If you or anyone you know has these symptoms, you have to consider it an illness that has to be treated and managed promptly.

Chapter 2: How BDD Is Diagnosed

BDD can be diagnosed with the help of medical and psychiatric tests. Therapists can diagnose it through its displayed symptoms, based on the American's Psychiatric Association of the Diagnostic and Statistical Manual of Mental Disorders (DSM-IV) (refer to Chapter 1). Here are the different methods to diagnose BDD.

1. **Symptoms through personal history**

    The psychologist or psychiatrist conducts a behavioral assessment through interview, questionnaires and exercises. The person's symptoms, answers, and behavior are then evaluated. For the sake of the accuracy of the evaluation, the person must be honest in answering the questions included in it.

2. **Psychological tests**

    Aside from the interview and observation of the individual's behavior, the health specialist may also conduct psychological tests to determine whether the symptoms are caused by other types of mental disorders, such as

Obsessive Compulsive Disorder (OCD), Asperger's Syndrome, or similar disorders.

3. **Physical exams (PE)**

   A health specialist will examine the person's body for any physical indications of BDD. This can be the marks of a series of aesthetic surgeries, multiple eyelash implants, excessive facial treatments, skin injury due to picking, and similar indications of extreme preoccupation with one's appearance.

4. **Laboratory exams**

   Diagnostic laboratory exams may be ordered by the health specialist to confirm his diagnosis. These tests can be Complete Blood Count or Hormone Function tests (Thyroid Function Test, Adrenal Function, and Progesterone or Testosterone Tests). The laboratory tests will rule out conditions associated with some metabolic illnesses, such as hyper- and hypothyroidism, hyper- and hypoadrenalism, and increased or decreased levels of gonadal hormones—progesterone and testosterone.

5. Neuroimaging

It has been reported that persons with BDD show a more fragile connection of the brain's orbitofrontal cortex with that of the amygdala. However, a broader and more comprehensive study has to be conducted to specifically establish the validity of this data.

These methods are enough to establish the diagnosis of BDD. If in doubt, always ask for a second opinion from another health specialist. As the saying goes, *"Two heads are better than one."*

Chapter 3: Behavioral Treatment Techniques and Medications

Since BDD is a mental illness, the treatment focuses more on behavioral techniques. The following are common treatment methods for BDD.

1. **Cognitive Behavioral Therapy (CBT)**

    This method deals with a series of sessions conducted between the therapist or health specialist with the BDD individual until the expected behavior is attained. This is accomplished by the therapist helping the individual change the way she thinks and behaves. This is due to the fact that the state of mind of an individual customarily dictates how she would behave. A positive frame of mind will help elicit healthy behavior, and can help the person cope with her disorder.

    The most common CBT is the graded Exposure and Response Prevention technique. With this technique, the person is gradually exposed to her fears until she is able to react normally without resorting to her usual repetitive response or BDD ritual. This can last from 5 months, up to 1 year or even a lifetime, depending on the severity of the disorder. A weekly or biweekly 50-minute visit must be scheduled for prompt intervention. Evidently, this is the general protocol, but this can be modified to suit the person's behavioral patterns.

On the other hand, Cognitive Restructuring is another CBT method where the person's thought processes are restructured positively to prevent focusing on the perceived flaws. The therapist has to model the treatment on the person's specific behavior.

2. **Psychodynamic Psychotherapy**

This method relies on the revelation of the unconscious mind of the patient (person with BDD) to resolve issues about her conscious actions. It is believed that when the conflicts of the unconscious mind are revealed and coped with, the symptoms of BDD will also disappear.

3. Medications

In severe cases, the doctor may opt to couple the CBT with therapeutic drugs, such as antidepressants referred to as Selective Serotonin Reuptake Inhibitors (SSRI).

SSRI are drugs that increase the secretion of serotonin, which is responsible for the reliable transmission of nerve impulses. An example of SSRI is fluoxetine. Fluoxetine can be taken daily for a period of 1 year or as needed. The drug should not be given unnecessarily to persons who are below 30 years old because this can worsen suicidal tendencies. The drug should only be administered to younger people, under the supervision of a competent clinician or doctor.

Side effects of SSRI:

- Nausea
- Headaches
- Fatigue
- Increased propensity to suicidal thoughts, especially in teenagers

Other medications can also be given, according to whatever symptoms the person displays. These drugs always require a doctor's prescription. It's important that you are aware of the fact that they are dangerous drugs that can cause serious side effects, if used improperly.

Chapter 4: Home Therapies and Interventions

Home interventions can be useful for persons afflicted with BDD, and family members can pitch in to lend moral support and encouragement. To help you more with BDD issues, here are some home interventions you can apply.

1. Discuss the pros and cons of her behavior

Before you can help the person change her behavior, she has to know why. You can let her understand by explaining the condition to her in simple terms that she can comprehend. If you have already consulted a health specialist, then you just have to inform her that your activity is a home intervention that can facilitate her treatment. After you have carefully explained BDD, you can now let her perform these simple steps.

- Let her prepare a logbook.

- In the logbook, instruct her to write down what she thinks are her BDD-related behavior.

- On the opposite side of each behavior, she has to write down the pros and cons of that particular behavior.

- Give her enough time to do it. Don't rush her. She can spend an entire day, or two if necessary, doing this activity.

- After her list is completed, ask her which of the behaviors she would want to retain, based on her assessment of the pros and cons.

- If she has done it correctly, all the items that she has listed will be considered as cons/disadvantages.

- Let her then suggest some specific actions that she can take to correct or get rid of the cons.

- The specific actions that she suggests will be her assigned task for the week. She can pick one or two positive behavior(s) and implement them until they become part of her natural behavior.

2. **Motivate her to cure her condition**

   She must be self-motivated to succeed in curing, or coping with, her illness. You can motivate her by explaining the benefits she can attain, such as being able to hang out with friends, having more self-confidence and living a normal life, etc.

3. **Show that you accept her through your actions**

   Whatever the progress of her treatment, you have to show that you accept her as part of the family. All family members must treat her with respect and dignity. A person's self-worth increases when her family members accept and respect her. She must also learn how to accept herself. Acceptance must come from the inside. Let her understand that everyone has flaws and these flaws are part of who she is as a person.

4. **Give her constant reassurance**

Reassuring her constantly will also boost her self-worth and self-confidence. This will help decrease her need to perform repetitive actions that worsen her BDD. A pat on the back and some words of encouragement are simple but effective ways to do so.

5. **Prevent her from doing rituals**

You have to be aware that rituals or repetitive actions are symptoms of BDD, and so should be avoided at all times. When the person starts staring at the mirror several times a day, you must remind her gently that it's a symptom; hence, she should avoid it. When you notice her picking at her skin, remind her that it's a BDD trait and that she should stop. It will be difficult at first, but eventually, she will be more aware of these rituals and will avoid them herself.

6. **Strengthen relationships**

   Strive to strengthen her relationships, because this will aid in minimizing the occurrence of the symptoms of BDD. Strengthening relationships can increase a person's self-worth. When she feels that she is accepted in spite of her flaws, she will be motivated to cope, and eventually get rid of her BDD.

7. **Emphasize her positive traits**

   She lacks self-confidence, so you have to assist her in gaining self-confidence by stressing her positive traits. If she insists she has flaws, point out that no one is perfect, but each has endearing qualities. You can point out some of her specific traits that she should be proud of, so she becomes aware of them and develops an optimistic attitude towards herself. Being an optimist is a crucial factor in the successful treatment of BDD.

8. **Inculcate optimism**

   Having a positive frame of mind is crucial when coping with BDD. It's important that the person thinks positively in order to overcome her disorder. It can be difficult becoming an optimist when one has been a pessimist all their life. But it can be done with persistence. Create scenarios and allow her to practice optimism.

Example A

- A shower of rain is seen negatively by some people. Let her observe the positive things about the rain for 30 minutes.

- Instruct her to write down these positive thoughts in the logbook.

- Discuss with her these positive thoughts. Why did she categorize them as positive? Inculcate in her mind that there's always something positive about any given situation.

Example B

- During rush hour when traffic is at a standstill, allow her to observe what's happening around her for 30 minutes.

- Instruct her to write down the positive things she has observed in the logbook.

- Discuss her observations. Why did she categorize them as positive? Talk with her to know more about her thoughts, so you can direct them accordingly.

- Let her realize that while lots of people would panic and get stressed out during traffic jams and similar incidents, it's her choice to remain calm and focus on the positive things. Let her learn that it's a matter of choice, and she can ultimately make the right and positive choice with constant practice.

- However, before you can help her, you must also be an optimist yourself. So, what's good about being caught in a traffic jam during rush hours? Well, you can take a breather and be able to perform your breathing exercises inside the car or bus. You can also have the time to read a page of a book or scan the newspaper. Things that you don't usually have the time for. You will also have the time to call your family members and bond with them, while waiting for the traffic to move. There are countless positive things that you can both perceive.

9. Reassure her of her appearance

Her appearance is of utmost importance to her, so you have to keep reassuring her that her appearance is good, and that whatever minor flaws she has are part of who she really is. Positive statements, such as: "Your dimples are cute.", "Your curls are pretty awesome!", "Your eyes are the most wonderful eyes I've ever seen.", "Your voice is sexy", can help significantly boost her confidence in her appearance. However, be sincere in your praise. People can immediately detect if you're just buttering them up. That's why it's essential to pick a genuine trait that is positive about them, so you can give praise honestly and sincerely.

If you can't find a positive physical trait, then you can focus on her character. What's good about the person's traits? Surely, there will always be something good in every person. A person with BDD typically lacks self-confidence, so focusing on her strengths will boost her self-confidence and help her cope with her BDD.

10. Reward her for any progress

Motivate her more by rewarding her whenever she is able to avoid doing the repetitive actions. You will have to be creative in thinking of ways to reward her wisely. Don't give money as a reward, but rather think of a fruitful and educational activity she can enjoy, and then do it together. Examples are: going on a fieldtrip to a space lab, picnicking, or going swimming.

There are various ways you can draw her away from focusing on her appearance. You will have to be ingenious in thinking of ways to make her behave positively. Remember to consider her likes and hobbies when planning these activities. If you are the one afflicted with BDD, then you will do well following the pointers given here to achieve the same results—and use good judgement in rewarding yourself too!

Chapter 5: Self-Assessment of BDD

You can assess yourself or another person to determine whether either one of you has BDD. You can easily know if you have BDD by observing any of the symptoms presented in Chapter 1. But to help you in coming to a correct conclusion, here are specific questions you can answer.

Ask yourself the following questions:

1. Do I focus on my minor flaws so much that it makes me afraid to socialize?

2. Do I have difficulty in deciding what to wear, even during ordinary occasions?

3. Do I feel extremely distressed when I notice a tiny pimple on my face?

4. Do I take a mirror with me when I go out and look at myself several times a day?

5. Do I keep picking a pimple, even when the skin is damaged already?

6. Do I constantly comb my hair, even when it's not ruffled?

7. Do I want to undergo various cosmetic surgeries?

8. Do I think of myself as a "monster?"

9. Do I regard myself as ugly?

10. Do I hate mirrors so much that I barely look at myself in the mirror?

11. Do I spend hours styling my hair every day?

12. Do I keep picking at my eyebrows because they're not perfect?

13. Have I ever skipped school or work because of a minor physical defect?

14. Have I ever isolated myself in my room because of a minor physical defect?

15. Have I ever attacked someone because I thought they were talking about my appearance?

16. Do I constantly think of committing suicide because I think I'm ugly?

17. After I had my first plastic surgery, did I want to undergo another one to correct another physical flaw?

18. Am I preoccupied with my weight, even when I have a normal weight?

19. Am I preoccupied with my appearance and flaws that I have shirked responsibilities at home and at work?

20. Am I preoccupied with my flaws so much that I no longer care about anything else?

If you answered "yes" to 3 or more of these questions, it indicates that you may have BDD. It's time to consult a health specialist. You must also be aware that there may be other mental disorders that can occur together with your BDD.

If there are additional behaviors that do not fall in the BDD parameter mentioned here, you should inform the health specialist. This is the best option in order to rule out other conditions.

Don't take chances by concluding that the disorder will go away on its own. This is dangerous, especially with teenagers, who are more susceptible to suicidal thoughts. The afflicted person must follow a correct individualized treatment plan that is appropriate for her, which is designed by a competent therapist.

Chapter 6: Choosing an Appropriate Therapist

Choosing the right therapist is crucial to the success of the BDD treatment. Hence, you must choose a therapist or health specialist only after careful deliberation. Here are some pointers you have to consider.

1. **The therapist must be licensed, competent and have had proper experience in treating BDD patients.** Expertise is usually gained after exposure. It's best to choose an experienced therapist. You can ask friends or family members if they can recommend a therapist. Word-of-mouth is always the best way to find legitimate and competent professionals. It's because this type of advertisement comes from persons who were patients of that particular therapist.

2. **The therapist must possess a pleasing personality.** He/she must be easy to deal with, and be amiable and sincere. This will make the patient feel more comfortable. When she's comfortable, treatment can proceed smoothly. This is the reason why first

sessions are generally spent making the patient feel at ease and comfortable.

3. **The therapist must be an effective teacher.** If the therapist doesn't know how to teach, the treatment will not succeed. A teacher is a facilitator of learning. Learning new behaviors is a daunting task, but with a qualified "teacher", it can be relatively easy.

4. **The therapist must respect the person with BDD.** A therapist who doesn't respect his/her patient's rights and dignity will most likely fail in changing the person's behavior. If the therapist doesn't show respect, get out fast!

5. **The therapist must be able to motivate the person.** Self-motivation can be extremely demanding for a person with BDD, so the therapist must have the know-how on assisting the person to motivate herself.

6. **The therapist must know how to document the sessions in an organized manner.** Questionnaires, session results, interviews, and records must be readily

available at all times, so that progress can be monitored accurately.

7. **The therapist must inspire trust.** The patient will not be able to open up about her thoughts if she doesn't trust her therapist. So, the therapist must be trustworthy and be able to inspire trust.

8. **The therapist must have a positive outlook.** Choose a therapist that is optimistic about life. This is one of the important attitudes needed in the treatment of BDD. The BDD patient herself can benefit greatly with a positive outlook; she can be motivated to change for the better.

9. **The therapist must be flexible.** Flexibility is needed under special circumstances if the patient becomes unruly or hard to manage. If the therapist operates only by the book, he/she may not be able to adjust to each individual's needs. BDD therapy must be individualized.

10. **The therapist must have a sense of humor.** Humor can dispel awkward moments, and can

put the patient at ease. You could get well more quickly when your health specialist is smiling and has a sense of humor. Who would like to be treated by a smug-faced person? Just looking at the therapist's face, the patient's condition could worsen.

These are the major traits that you should look for when choosing a therapist. Understandably, you want the therapist to be a perfect match with the patient. Hence, the patient should help you in choosing her own therapist.

Chapter 7: Additional Tips for Coping with the Disorder

Coping with BDD requires patience and persistence. To cope with the disorder, the negative behavior, rituals or repetitive actions must be avoided to break the habit. It can be a gargantuan task to accomplish. So, here are some valuable tips to help you achieve your objective.

1. **If you feel conscious or bad about a physical flaw—that's normal.** Don't immediately think you have BDD. But if you feel extremely distressed because of it, and you can't focus on your usual daily activities, then you might have BDD.

2. **BDD can affect any age group.** However, it's predominant in teenagers and adolescents, or young adults. Reportedly, 1 in every 100 persons is afflicted with BDD. That number is increasing, so make sure the young adult in your family is free from this debilitating disorder by observing her closely. It's easier to treat the condition during its early stages. Take note that there is also an increasing number of teen suicides due to BDD.

3. **If the symptoms persist, consult a health specialist.** If the behavior of the person doesn't improve, you have to consult a health specialist, a psychologist, a psychiatrist, a doctor, or a therapist, depending on the symptoms observed. If you have the financial capability, you should consult a team of health specialists.

4. **BDD can be mistaken as OCD.** The two disorders have some similar symptoms, such as repetitive behavior and suicidal tendencies. They are not the same though, so you will have to know the symptoms yourself to help the specialist arrive at the correct diagnosis.

5. **There should be rapport between therapist and the BDD afflicted person.** This is important for the treatment to succeed. Hence, if the patient dislikes her therapist, even after several sessions, you have to find another therapist that she can trust and feel comfortable with.

6. **BDD is chronic, so be ready for the long haul.** As mentioned earlier, patience and persistence are needed to cope with this disorder. But here's good news, the disorder

can be managed and treated properly with the correct methods.

7. **Support groups can play an important role in BDD treatment.** Having a support group with people suffering from the same disorder can help a lot in coping with BDD. If the person finds out that she is not alone, this will give her more self-confidence so that she can deal with it. There are various groups online that she can enlist in. But a local support group is recommended because she can participate in activities with the other members.

Here are online support groups:

- Body Dysmorphic Disorder & Body Image Clinic, Los Angeles
http://body-dysmorphic-disorder.supportgroups.com/

- Body Dysmorphic Disorder Clinic
http://bddclinic.com/bddtreatment/supportgroups/

8. **The cognitive and behavioral methods in CBT are effective for young adults.** This means that the therapists not only have to guide the person to behave appropriately, they must also allow her to acquire new information or knowledge to deal with her disorder.

9. **Cosmetic surgery can create new problems.** This is because, no matter how her appearance turns out after the surgery, a person with BDD will always find defects in how she looks.

10. **To cure or manage a person with BDD, her attitude, way of thinking, and behavior must be changed first.** When she changes her attitude to a more positive one and changes the way she thinks, a normal behavior will consequently follow.

11. **Each individual has a unique personality.** Therefore, the CBT must be patterned along the lines of the individual's personality. This will increase the chances of success in treating the condition.

12. **Efficacy of drug treatment must be monitored.** This is imperative so that the concentration of the drug administered is effective in treating the disease. In most cases, a trial period of 3 to 4 months is implemented to ensure successful treatment.

13. **There can be other disorders that can co-exist with BDD.** Some of these are OCD, social phobia, compulsive skin picking (dermatillomania), excessive hair pulling (trichotillomania), personality disorders and eating disorders. In such a special case, the treatment strategy must include the co-existing disorder.

14. **Scheduled treatments and therapy sessions must be strictly complied with.** If the treatment schedule is not followed strictly, this can disrupt the patient's progress and management.

15. **The therapist must act as a teacher or a coach.** Aside from having good rapport with the patient, the therapist must know how to teach and guide the person to acquire a positive behavior.

You can improvise if you have to, but always keep these valuable pointers in mind and use these tips to succeed in coping with BDD.

Conclusion

Treating BDD and coping with it is a doable task. With the correct attitude and the determination to succeed, you can do it. Whoever the patient may be, you, your child, or a friend, the methods presented in this book are simple to follow and can be implemented in all cases.

Keep in mind that the earlier the treatment starts, the better the chances of the person being able to overcome BDD. However, be alert to the serious symptoms of the disease, such as aggression and suicidal tendencies. You have to monitor the person constantly to detect danger signals. If you have observed these serious behavioral patterns, it's best to report the matter immediately to the therapist or health specialist.

Reinforce the treatment by doing your home interventions regularly. The therapist will give some assignments, so you must ensure that these are done correctly. In this regard, family members have a vital role in helping the person cope with her BDD. Each member must know what to do and how to respond given certain BDD situations.

The success of coping with BDD lies in the cooperation of all the parties concerned: the person, the therapist or health specialists, the family, and the other people around the patient. Whether you or someone else is in need of help, by opening up to those who care or by facilitating this kind of team effort to support the affected person, you will be making this enormous task seem more surmountable.

Finally, I'd like to thank you for purchasing this book! If you found it helpful, I'd greatly appreciate it if you'd take a moment to leave a review on Amazon. Thank you!

Printed in Great Britain
by Amazon